Date: 9/23/14

Dirty Jobs

Coal Miner

Pamela McDowell

www.av2books.com

AV² provides enriched content that supplements and complements this book. Weigl's AV² books strive to create inspired learning and engage young minds in a total learning experience.

Your AV² Media Enhanced books come alive with...

Audio
Listen to sections of the book read aloud.

Key Words
Study vocabulary, and complete a matching word activity.

Video
Watch informative video clips.

Quizzes
Test your knowledge.

Go to **www.av2books.com**, and enter this book's unique code.

BOOK CODE

P93945

Embedded Weblinks
Gain additional information for research.

Slide Show
View images and captions, and prepare a presentation.

AV² **by Weigl** brings you media enhanced books that support active learning.

Try This!
Complete activities and hands-on experiments.

... and much, much more!

Published by AV² by Weigl
350 5ᵗʰ Avenue, 59ᵗʰ Floor
New York, NY 10118

Websites: www.av2books.com   www.weigl.com

Library of Congress Control Number: 2014934638

ISBN 978-1-4896-0986-1 (hardcover)
ISBN 978-1-4896-0987-8 (Softcover)
ISBN 978-1-4896-0988-5 (Single-user eBook)
ISBN 978-1-4896-0989-2 (Multi-user eBook)

Printed in the United States of America in North Mankato, Minnesota.
1 2 3 4 5 6 7 8 9 0   18 17 16 15 14

032014
WEP150314

Project Coordinator: Aaron Carr
Designer: Mandy Christiansen

Every reasonable effort has been made to trace ownership and to obtain permission to reprint copyright material. The publishers would be pleased to have any errors or omissions brought to their attention so that they may be corrected in subsequent printings.

Weigl acknowledges Getty Images and iStockPhoto as primary image suppliers for this title.

Contents

What Is a Coal Miner?

Coal miners are workers who remove coal from deep underground. They clean and sort the coal before it can be used by power stations to make electricity. Most coal mines run 24 hours a day to make enough coal to fill the demand for electricity. Hundreds of coal miners work at different tasks in each mine.

Coal miners work all over the world. The top five coal-mining countries are China, the United States, India, Australia, and South Africa. In 2011, the United States produced more than 1 billion tons (907 million metric tons) of coal. The United States uses most of this coal, sending only about 15 percent to other countries.

One Mine, Many Jobs.

Just one coal mine can have many jobs. Some miners **specialize** in a skill. These miners may be blasters, drillers, backfillers, or heavy equipment operators. Other people who work in coal mines include engineers, surveyors, and safety managers.

91,611 people work as coal miners in the United States.

Coal produces **42 percent** of U.S. energy.

People have used coal as a fuel for more than 3,000 years.

Coal miners work together to provide the world with the fuel it needs.

Where They Work

Twenty-five states in the United States mine coal. These coal mines are far away from cities and often even far away from small towns. Coal miners may work in pits above ground or in deep tunnels underground.

Working underground can be a dark and dangerous job.

Surface Mining

Coal is often near Earth's surface. If the coal is less than 200 feet (60 meters) deep, dirt is scraped away to reach it in a process called surface mining or open-cut mining. More than two-thirds of the mines in the United States are surface mines. Here, miners work outside.

Underground Mining

If the coal is more than 200 feet (60 m) below the surface, miners must dig tunnels to reach it. Some underground mines are 1,000 feet (305 m) deep. Miners first ride an elevator down to the tunnels. Then, the miners take an underground train to get to the work site. Traffic lights, such as those used on city streets, help the trains run safely. Miners in underground mines must be ready to work in dark, tight spaces.

Surface mining poses great risk to the surrounding area. Mining companies must plan how they will control pollution and restore the land after mining is complete.

A Dirty Job

Coal mining is a dirty job. In modern coal mines, machines do much of the work. These machines create a lot of dirt and dust. Miners cannot avoid getting dirty as they work in the middle of all this dirt.

Coal Mining Dangers

Mining is a dangerous job. Miners working with large equipment must be alert and careful to avoid being hurt. Supervisors receive special training to keep everyone in the mine safe.

The biggest danger for coal miners is the dust made by their work. A miner's lungs may be damaged by breathing the dust. The miner will have trouble breathing and will cough frequently. There is no treatment for this condition, known as "Black Lung" disease.

Coal miners rely on both machinery and each other to get the job done.

> Safety is a top priority in a coal mine. Workers look out for each other as they work and travel throughout the mine.

Hard Hat

The first hard hats were made from layers of canvas. The canvas was glued together and painted with a layer of **shellac**. The hats had a candle or lamp attached to the front. Later, hard hats were made of aluminum, fiberglass, and injected thermoplastic.

In 1919, Edward D. Bullard made the first hard hat.

> Coal miners must take care to protect themselves from the dust in coal mines.

A 20-pound
(9-kilogram) weight dropped from 2 feet (0.6 m) would not break the canvas hard hat.

The carbide lamp, a lamp attached to the helmet to give better light than candles, only lasted about 4 hours before it had to be refueled.

All in a Day's Work

Coal mines run both day and night, so miners work in shifts. A nine- or ten-hour shift may start early in the morning, in the afternoon, or in the evening. Underground miners begin their day by checking in. Then, they move to the wash house to change into work clothes and get their safety gear. Partway through their shift, the miners will take a break to eat the lunch or dinner they have brought with them. They eat at the work site in a spot called the "dinner hole." At the end of the day, they ride back to the surface. The miners shower and check out before going home.

"I have worked underground most of my life," says Tom, the Lead Safety Auditor at a coal mine in Alabama. "More than 350 people work underground in our mine. Being a coal miner can be demanding and dangerous. Working in tunnels with only a light on my cap is very different from working outside in the sunlight. Coal miners are skilled workers who supply a product that is important to the world. Coal mining is a good paying job, and I am proud to be a coal miner."

Working underground is not for everyone, but coal miners take great pride in their work. Many men and women come from generations of coal miners.

Coal-fired power stations make **40 percent** of the world's electricity.

A rail car can carry about six tons (5.4 metric tons) of processed, or cleaned, coal.

From the Mine to the Home

Taking the coal from the mine is just the first step in the course that coal travels to become power or products. Power stations use coal to create energy. Factories use coal to make items people use every day. People and companies are not able to immediately use the coal from mines. The coal must first go through a process before it is shipped out to be used.

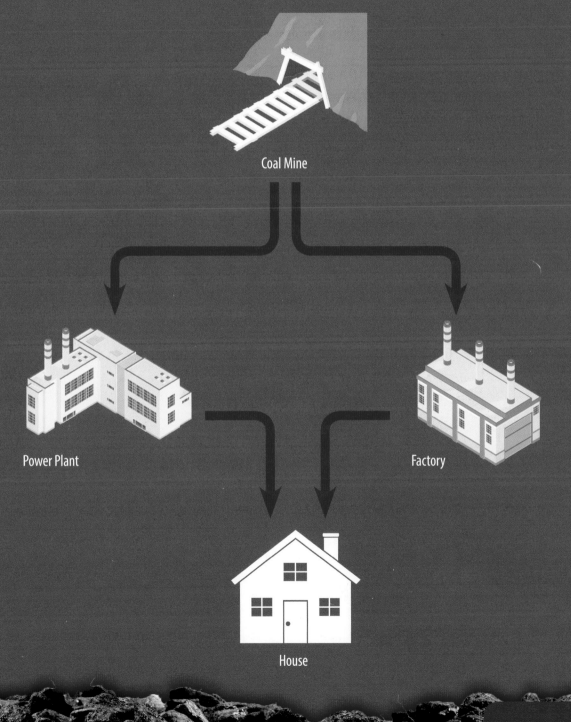

Coal Mine

Power Plant

Factory

House

Staying Safe

There are many hazards in a coal mine. Explosions and fires can happen, but miners work hard to reduce these risks. Standard safety equipment for a coal miner can include:

Gas Detector and Respirator

Some dangerous gases do not have an odor, and a miner might not know he or she is breathing poisonous air. A gas detector measures the gases in the air and lets the miner know when dangerous fumes are present. The miner can put a respirator, called a self-rescuer, over his or her nose and mouth for clean air until reaching a safe area.

Work Boots

Boots with steel toes protect a miner's feet from falling objects and heavy machinery. Boots provide grip if the work site is wet or if the ground is rough.

Safety First

Coal miners must wear safety gear when they are working in the mine. Supervisors check for face protection and heavy clothing. They also check the **ventilation** in the mine to make sure the air is safe. Supervisors must track workers carefully. It is important to know where every person is working in the mine.

Helmet

Miners wear helmets to protect themselves from falling objects, such as rocks. Straps inside the helmet absorb the impact and reduce injury. Helmets have lights or lamps built in. Face shields and video cameras can also be attached.

Safety glasses, earplugs, gloves

Safety glasses protect the miner's eyes from coal dust and bits of rock. Earplugs protect the miner's hearing when using noisy equipment. Gloves protect the miner's hands from sharp machinery.

Tools of the Trade

Coal miners use some of the biggest machines in the world. With these machines, a miner today can produce three times more coal per hour than a miner did in 1978. The machines are complicated and require special training to use. There are different kinds of machines for underground and surface mining.

Shovel
This machine, also called an excavator, removes dirt or coal from a surface mine. The driver sits in the cab, which can rotate. The driver uses controls inside the shovel to move the long arm and scoop with the bucket.

Continuous Cutter
This machine has teeth made of tungsten carbide, a combination of metals that is very hard. These teeth scrape coal from the underground mine. The continuous cutter can work in tight places. It can be operated by remote control if necessary.

Blasthole Drills
Often, surface miners must remove a layer of rock in order to reach the coal. A blasthole drill creates a series of holes as it moves along the rock. A worker called a blaster puts explosives in these holes to break the rock apart. Then, the shovel and dragline can scoop up the rock.

Longwall Cutter

This machine cuts blocks of coal from the walls of an underground tunnel. It moves forward on its own. The coal falls onto a conveyor belt that takes it to the surface. The longwall cutter is 800 feet (240 m) wide and 5 to 10 (1.5 to 3 m) tall. It will cut walls up to 12,000 feet (3,650 m) long. That is equal to the length of 40 football fields.

Dragline

This may be the world's biggest machine. The dragline removes dirt to reach the coal in surface mining. The bucket that scoops the dirt is the size of a two-car garage.

Then

In the past, children as young as eight years old worked in coal mines. In 1902, a new law said that workers, usually boys, must be at least 14 years old. Sometimes, children worked 10 hours a day, 6 days a week. They did dangerous jobs in the mines. Pickers could lose fingers in the machinery as they sorted coal. Spraggers could be crushed by a mine car full of coal as they tried to slow it down. Grumpy mules could injure mule drivers as they traveled through the tunnels.

Now

Today, laws focus on the safety and training of coal miners. Some states require workers to be at least 18 years old to work for a mining company. Machines produce and process more coal faster than a whole team of men could 100 years ago.

The Coal Miner's Role

While much about coal mining has changed, coal miners still play a key role in the production of electric energy. Miners no longer use **pickaxes** and shovels to remove coal by hand. Today's machines may be more efficient, but they have not replaced the miners. People must run the machinery at every step. Miners still spend their workday down in the tunnels or in the pits of a surface mine.

"It's a dirty job, but someone has to do it."

Processing Coal

As coal is cut from the wall of a mine, it falls onto a conveyor belt. This belt carries the coal to the processing plant. The coal then drops into a tank. Rocks and dirt sink to the bottom of the tank, and the coal floats. Another machine spins the coal dry. Another machine crushes the coal so the pieces are the same size. Trains take the coal to power stations all over North America. There, coal is burned to boil water and make steam. Steam spins a propeller. The energy from the spinning propeller is then used to create electricity.

Even with machines to do the heavy lifting, dedicated workers are still the driving force of the coal mining industry.

Coal and the Environment

Power stations that burn coal produce pollution such as carbon dioxide and sulfur. Removing sulfur from the coal before it is burned stops the sulfur from going into the air. Mining companies try to remove all of the sulfur before burning the coal. A device called a scrubber cleans the smoke before it is released into the outside air. Years ago, miners sent leftover ash from burned coal to landfills. Now the ash is recycled. Roads and cement are made from this ash. Ocean reefs for marine animals are also made from recycled ash.

The amount of sulfur dioxide released into the air has been reduced by **71 percent** in the U.S. since 1999.

Scientists believe there is enough coal in the United States to last at least 300 years.

Scrubbers can remove **90 to 97** percent of sulfur dioxide emissions.

Becoming a Coal Miner

A person must have the right skills and attitude to spend most of each day underground. A high school diploma is usually required to work as a coal miner. In some states, workers must complete an **apprenticeship** course and exam. The course is 40 to 80 hours of training. After working for six months, the apprentice can take a test to become fully **certified**. A worker who trains in explosives, machine repair, or first aid may be hired more quickly. A worker with specialized skills may also receive higher pay.

Some workers may complete a college degree program in engineering, surveying, geology, math, or science. Skilled professionals are needed to operate the complex machinery used in mines. The chart below shows the yearly income for different positions in coal mining.

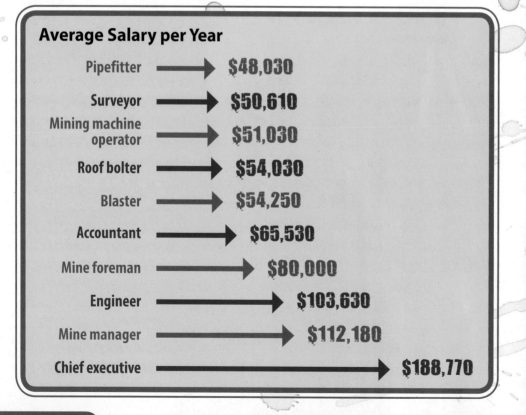

Average Salary per Year

Position	Salary
Pipefitter	$48,030
Surveyor	$50,610
Mining machine operator	$51,030
Roof bolter	$54,030
Blaster	$54,250
Accountant	$65,530
Mine foreman	$80,000
Engineer	$103,630
Mine manager	$112,180
Chief executive	$188,770

Coal miners operate like an underground family. Many young miners learn the trade from older, more experienced workers.

Is This Career for You?

A career as a coal miner is not easy. The work is dusty and noisy. Miners have to work in tight, dark spaces. While this work can sometimes be dangerous, a career as a coal miner provides an important product that every person relies on in some way. Without coal, there would be almost no electric power for factories, businesses, and homes. Coal mining is a rewarding career that helps the world work.

✓ **Training**
Only miners who have had proper training can enter a mine. The company may provide training in operating heavy machines and working in tight spaces. Safety training is always important.

✓ **Education**
A miner may need more than a high school diploma. Completing a college or university program can provide the skills needed.

✓ **Application**
To apply for a job at a coal mine, contact the mining company. Many advertise on the internet or in newspapers.

Career Connections

Plan your coal mining career with this activity. Follow the instructions outlined in the steps to complete the process of becoming a coal miner.

1. If you live near a coal mine, speak to a coal miner. This person can answer your questions and give you an inside look into the position.

2. Visit a job fair or university career center to find out more information about working in the coal mining industry.

3. Work on your resumé. A good resumé highlighting your strongest skills can attract the attention of potential employers.

4. Call or write to a coal mining company. Say that you are interested in a job as a coal miner and ask for advice on how to apply.

1. Decide if you have the personality and attitude for coal mining. If you do not mind a dirty job, can work in tight spaces, and are in good physical shape, this may be the job for you.

2. Consider the skills you will need. Look for schools that train mining apprentices. Having a valid driver's license and first aid certificate will be a bonus.

3. Contact employers for requirements. Get in touch with mining companies and find out what they are looking for from potential applicants.

4. Apply for the position and arrange for an interview. If you are successful, come to the interview with knowledge of the industry and your skills.

Quiz

1. How much coal did the United States produce in 2011?

2. What are the two different types of coal mines?

3. What causes "Black Lung" disease?

4. What gas could cause an explosion in a mine?

5. How much of the world's electricity is made using coal?

6. Name three pieces of safety equipment a coal miner must have.

7. What does the dragline do at a surface mine?

8. Why is coal burned at power stations?

9. What removes sulfur and carbon dioxide from the smoke as coal is being burned?

10. How many hours of training does an apprentice coal miner need?

Answers:
1. 1 billion tons (907 million metric tons)
2. Underground and surface
3. Breathing in coal dust
4. Methane
5. 40 percent
6. Helmet, work boots, respirator, gas detector, safety glasses, ear plugs, heavy gloves
7. Removes the layer of earth to get to the coal
8. To make steam to turn a propeller to make electricity
9. Scrubbers
10. 40 to 80 hours

Key Words

apprenticeship: basic training in special skills

certified: trained and tested as having the skills needed

pickaxes: tools with wooden handles and metal heads that have sharp blades on one end and sharp points on the other end

shellac: a liquid that is painted on and hardens as it dries

specialize: to focus on one area of work or skill

ventilation: when fresh air is allowed in and stale air is released

Index